Farm GIRL

RUDYARD THURBER

BANYAN·TREE·PRESS

FarmGIRL

Copyright © 2012 by Rudyard Thurber

All rights reserved. No part of this book may be reproduced in any form by any electronic or mechanical means including photocopying, recording, or information storage and retrieval without permission in writing from the author.

ISBN-13:
Library of Congress Control Number:

Banyan Tree Press
www.banyantreepress.com
Englewood, Colorado
Austin, Texas
Cover/Interior by: DPMediaPro.com
Printed in U.S.A

Table of Contents

Dedication VII

Just So—So Stories

Grandma Said 3
The Lilac Bush 5
Slide Rule 11
Shift Work 13
Fantasy 15
Implosion 17
Weaveball Redux 19
Double H 21
Farm Girl 23
Gerrymeandering 29
Muscle Memory 31
DumbWriter 33
Time's Up 35
Eureka! 37
Comes Around 39
Brushes 41
Dodger Blue(s) 43
Simon Sings 45
Dropout 47
Joe M. 51
NCFF 53
Ends and Odds 55

Nuances
- Last Stop ... 60
- Demarcation ... 61
- Pride and Joy ... 62
- Goose P**p ... 63
- Red Velvet Love ... 64
- Acolyte ... 65
- Tarnished Man ... 66
- Bubble Bath ... 67
- Adrift ... 68
- Hard Times ... 69
- Fight or Flight ... 70
- Squall ... 71
- Hot Cold Hot ... 72
- Exiting ... 73
- Bridle Sweet ... 74
- Torque ... 75

Needs Music
- Whispering ... 78
- Panhandler Blues ... 79
- Kettle. Bell Rung. ... 80
- Rockets ... 82
- Dry Hole ... 83
- Wait For You ... 84

About the Author ... 87
- Interview of Bobbin Raye Ballou ... 88

Also by this author:
Rack and Wruin

Dedication

This work is honored to salute Gloria, Barbie, Maggie, my awesome sister—Gypsy Jo, and all the marvelous farm girls who intersected my life in some way. May the world understand and appreciate the wonderful impact farmgirls have on our society.

Just So—So Stories

Grandma Said

We have been blessed with an abundance of wonderful granddaughters. Not an overabundance, just a perfect abundance and, of course, they are all beautiful and brainy.

One such granddaughter I will call "Bibi" in this, a true story.

When Bibi was still a teenager, she held a job a few miles from home. It was a night job so it was dark when she would get off work.

One night, she didn't come at the usual time. One hour went by, then two, then several more. This was before navigation systems in cars.

In the wee hours of morning, she called and told her dad she had gotten lost and was in a town called Hector, about sixty miles west of the town where she lived and worked. Her father told her to wait there and he would come and lead her home.

When he got there, he asked, naturally enough, why she just kept driving without knowing where she was headed. She answered just as naturally and without any artificiality,

"Well, Grandma always says all roads lead to home."

The Lilac Bush

When his wife came home from her afternoon walk, she told quite an incredible story. At an intersection near their home, on some parkland, stands a lilac bush. It is about twenty feet square and about ten feet high.

Veronica (his wife) stated that she saw a man walk up to the bush, part some branches, and then enter it. She waited, in somewhat of a stunned state, for the man to re-emerge but he never did. At first, when he was walking up to the bush, she thought all he was going to do was just either smell the flowers or break off a sprig and take it with him. She never expected to see him enter the bush.

Melvin (the husband) cogitated on this development for a few minutes and finally offered "Maybe it's a homeless person using the bush for his domicile."

That pretty much concluded the discussion on the topic and they each went about doing their own things; Veronica making supper and Melvin continuing to watch baseball on the television.

A couple of days later, when Veronica had gone with a busload from church to a casino, Melvin found himself home alone and a little bored. It was then he remembered the tale of the lilac bush. He decided to check it out and went digging for the flashlight just in case.

He approached the bush from the same direction as the person Veronica had seen. At first, everything seemed normal. He found the opening where the man must have parted the branches and, likewise, entered the copse. He didn't have the flashlight on but dimly saw something that looked a little out of place in the center of the bush.

He turned on the flashlight and found himself looking at a circular wrought iron railing. An opening in the railing showed stairs descending. He grabbed onto the railing and started down.

After what seemed the equivalent of at least three flights, he came to a landing. He stepped off and noticed it was well lit. There were walkways and he chose one and started down the path. After walking a short way he heard a childlike voice say "Hi."

He turned around and saw a small girl.

"Hi. Who are you?"

"My name is Sarah. I'm to be your guide."

"My guide? Am I lost? Why do I need a guide?"

"You will soon see, Melvin."

"How do you know my name?"

"I was told it."

"I see. By whom?"

"You will soon know that also. Shall we begin the tour?"

"I guess so, Sarah.

"You might as well turn off your flashlight. You won't be needing it."

"Okay."

Sarah chose a path to the right and, taking Melvin's hand, started down it. After passing a couple more walkways she took one to the left and, shortly, they came to where there was some music. The live band, curiously peopled only with small children, was quite good. The drummer was especially talented and his solo was unforgettable.

Melvin had to ask "What is the drummer's name?"

"His name is Anger but everyone calls him 'Blur.'"

Melvin mused out loud "Interesting name, 'Anger.'"

"Yes," was all Sarah offered.

They moved on and came to a beautiful garden. Tending the garden were three small children. Melvin didn't think he had ever seen such a lovely array of plantings as this.

"This is truly beautiful, Sarah."

"Yes. They work very hard at their craft."

"What is this place, Sarah?"

"It's composed entirely of small children and extends around the world. We are all of a group we call joyhort."

By now they were near what appeared to be an artists' colony. Small children were painting on easels and the products were truly stunning.

Melvin stopped by an easel with a picture which he particularly liked. It was an oil painting of a church he recognized as one in his own town.

He turned to the artist and said "That is truly beautiful. What is your name?"

"Happy," she replied.

"How much is it?" he asked.

"I'm sorry, but it's not for sale."

"I see."

Melvin turned to Sarah and asked, "Why wouldn't she sell it to me?"

Sarah simply said, "Look around—do you see any place to spend money?"

"No. But, then, how do you all survive?"

"You come from a different paradigm, Melvin. We do not respect money here. But we are well taken care of."

As she said this they came upon what appeared to be a woodworking shop. They entered and the smell of sawdust was rampant. Everywhere one looked were children working on various woodworking projects.

Each of the projects Melvin looked at were masterful works. He marveled at one particular piece and said to its creator "This is truly beautiful. I wish I had your talent." The youthful craftsperson merely replied, "Thank you."

"Sarah—who are all these talented young people and why are they here? I know you said something about joy, but I'm afraid I missed the rest of it."

"I said we were all part of joyhort. That is short for joyless cohort. You see, Melvin, we all have the same thing in common—we are all unwanted children."

"What do you mean, 'unwanted'?"

"We were all aborted, Melvin."

Melvin felt like a truckload of bricks had landed on his chest. His mind was swirling and he couldn't seem to organize his thoughts. All of a sudden, the resistance in him melted and he softly said, "We did that early in our marriage. I had just been drafted and my wife wasn't working, and we felt like we couldn't afford a child at that time."

He continued: "It wasn't legal yet so we had to find a doctor who would ignore the law."

Sarah said, "Money is the most common reason we hear about as the motivation. Now do you see why we don't respect money down here?"

They continued walking while Melvin was in deep thought. Finally he asked: "So all the children come here to live instead of Heaven?"

"No. We come here to live until we've been given the Great Grace. Most of us need it three times but some only two."

"You've lost me, Sarah; what, exactly, is the 'Great Grace' and why the variation in times it is needed?"

Sarah patiently explained: "The Great Grace is the grace of forgiveness. When we are ready to forgive those who sent us here, we are given the opportunity, one by one with our mother, our father, and the doctor. In some cases, the father is not aware of us so we just have to forgive the mother and the doctor. The doctors are the hardest to forgive. Some of them think they are a step up from God and don't need forgiveness but we can't help that. We just forgive and move on."

"After we have truly forgiven, including in our hearts, we go to Heaven."

Melvin had a lot of questions and didn't know where to begin. "Why are some of the children named after pleasant words and others after troublesome ones?"

"Oh, that. We are allowed to choose our own names down here. Some choose names that reflect how they feel. Others choose ones that reflect how they would *like* to feel."

"And you chose the name of Sarah. Why?"

"I admire Sarah for her patience and faithfulness. I would like to have known her."

"Yes, Sarah, that is, indeed, a wise choice."

Melvin felt the need to compliment her, "I bet your parents would have been very proud of you."

"Thanks, Dad. And I forgive you."

Melvin felt his knees buckle.

"Oh, my…This is beyond anything I could imagine. You would have been our daughter!" At this he tried to embrace her, but she stepped back.

"If we both end up in Heaven, then you may hug me. For now, consider this: You and Veronica could have had a child almost at the beginning of your marriage. Sarah had to wait until near the end of hers."

"I understand," Melvin said unsure if he did or not. "I can't wait to tell Veronica."

"When you leave here you will not remember what has happened."

"Okay. Thank you for forgiving me, Sarah."

"Sarah—how do these children end up in their respective vocations?"

"Again, we are given a choice. You will find no politicians here nor any soldiers. The one we all disdain and the other we all sympathize with."

"And you chose to be a guide?" asked Melvin.

"No. I am your guide but my vocation is as a Catholic priest."

"But, women can't be priests, Sarah."
"Again, Melvin, you come from a different paradigm."

*****

Veronica came home and found Melvin sleeping on the couch again. She gently shook him into consciousness. "I'm home dear."

Melvin groggily replied, "How did it go, dear?"

"Oh. The usual."

Melvin replied, "I'm sorry to hear that."

Veronica asked Melvin "Why did you fall asleep with the flashlight in your hand?"

Confused, he looked at his hand which held the flashlight, studied it for a moment, shook his head and said, "I have no idea."

*****

Author's Note:

The story above is fiction but based on a real-life experience. One day my wife actually did come back from a walk and described the incident at the lilac bush near our home. The rest is pure speculation. Still, until someone actually checks out the bush, I would submit the story is as plausible as any. . .

Slide Rule

I miss Dizzy Dean.

As a kid growing up in a cultural wasteland, my one weekly joy was the Saturday Afternoon Baseball Game of the Week with Dizzy Dean and Pee Wee Reese.

Dizzy was probably the most compelling sports announcer ever. He was famously raspberried for saying things like "He slud halfway from third to home." but it all made sense to me. It was from Dizzy that I learned about "Texas Leaguers" and "the ol' blue darter."

Today, they make announcers semi-expert in multiple sports and the result is, mostly, abysmal. The only two two-sport announcers that were reasonably credible were the late Curt Gowdy and Pat Summerall.

Today, you will hear a guy who does football, covering a golf tournament saying something like ". . . and we all remember Brad hitting his third round tee shot into the rough on the seventeenth hole at Pinehurst in 1992."

Give me a break.

No one remembers and, furthermore, no one cares! Besides, it's just golf!

Thank goodness the powers that were didn't tamper with the notion that Dizzy was a (wonderful) one-trick pony!

Shift Work

Back in the mid 1960s, I worked for a major airplane manufacturer in the Seattle area. It was a lively time with the build-up of their small carrier, the design and development of a supersonic transport going on, and the advent of "jumbo" carriers all happening at the same time.

We worked all shifts and all hours to meet deadlines. Things were really dynamic. Once, at a plant by King County airfield, one unit changed managers in the middle of a shift.

This company tried to stay ahead of the management curve and, even in the 1960s, had implemented badges which were used to punch in and out. At this plant, during the staffing build-up, one person figured out to come in with one shift and punch in, then walk out without punching out with the crew leaving. He would then come back eight hours later with the next shift, punch in again (which, now amounted to punching *out*) and leave with the crew leaving at this time.

In all the confusion, he got by with this for almost a month.

With all the overtime we worked, it was easy to get punchy. One night we got off about three in the morning and when we came to the gate there were no security guards to let us out. Being so tired we didn't go looking for them but, instead, climbed over the fence and started walking to our cars.

About this time the guards showed up and tried to get us to come back to the guard house. My friends just kept walking but I, being a pleasant sort of person, figured I would at least give them the opportunity to apologize for being absent from their post so I went back. Dumb move. They took my badge.

Two days later I was reassigned to the jumbo jet facility up in Everett. This facility, about forty miles away and in a forty acre building, was a huge factory befitting its product.

The fuselage on this plane was so large we worked on it on three different layers. There was metal decking set up for this and, the key to success here, was to be on the third deck at the end of your shift because, for the last five to ten minutes, we always swept up. The decking had a pattern of holes in it so those below got bombarded.

I was reminded of this when I moved back to Minnesota. Someone mentioned to me that, in a town called Belle Plaine, stands a two story outhouse.

Try to get your mind around this. If someone is on the second floor being busy, would you want to be on the lower level? I just couldn't fathom it. Did so many people have to go to the bathroom at the same time in Belle Plaine that they had to do it in layers?

Eventually I saw the edifice and realized the wisdom of it. It is located behind the main house and there is a walkway from the second story of the house to the upper reaches of the outhouse. I suppose in the Twin Cities this would be called a skyway.

I still don't know if there is a functional unit in the lower level. Not sure I want to.

Fantasy

Fantasy is a world of ever-changing landscape. When I was a young guy, my fantasy was to live in either a gymnasium or a girl's dormitory. Later, of course, the fantasy was just the girl part.

In my mid-life adult years I did achieve one of the landmarks—the gymnasium. With an MBA in my possession, I found myself out of work and seriously struggling in the early nineties. I managed to get a room in the St. Paul Athletic Club (SPAC), an icon of the old days in St. Paul, which was failing also. A few bachelors inhabited this largely empty fourteen story building in the heart of downtown.

In later years, fantasy came to require my attention during both baseball and football seasons. Fantasy baseball and football became something to keep me interested in the seasons and reaffirm my management skills.

As I look back, fantasy baseball, especially, was important to me because, part of the management skill sets was trading players among the other teams in your league. This, I now realize, was an extension of my youth when we would trade baseball cards. Times have changed. When my son was younger I would buy him entire sets of cards (Hockey!) and there would be no bubblegum. How I miss the smell of that gum!

Fantasy is now so pervasive that one of my brothers wanted to do a fantasy NASCAR contest with me. NASCAR!

Fantasy football is now in full swing and, a sign of the times is this: My undefeated season came to a screeching halt this past weekend thanks to a team whose manager has the name "Michelle."

Is nothing sacred?

Implosion

In the center of town stands a building that has been there for over forty years. Now, a building is more than just concrete and steel. It is the sum of everything that has happened there over the years; it eventually will have a personality.

This particular building has seen business deals struck and deals fizzle. It has seen friendships form, alliances be created and modified, babies made, people die, crying and laughing.

It is a building I shared with a special friend. Also present were our mutual counselor, Mr. Ike, and MM and all the alliterative nicknames you gave me. More importantly, the building housed the bulk of my trust which I had placed in you.

One day, in my absence, you imploded the building. All was lost.

You placed the charges well.

In another building across town is an office. In a drawer in a filing cabinet in that office is the set of plans used to construct the building you imploded. You could take those plans, hire a general contractor, clear the rubble, and build another building on the same spot.

But it would be a different building.

I do not wish to create a new building. I have no more trust to donate. In a way, I died when the first building went down.

Weaveball Redux

In my previous volume (*Rack and Wruin*) I proposed a new game called "Weaveball." In the thesis, I postulated that nine players could bat in an inning and no one scores. I said that thinking it was the ultimate in extreme circumstances.

This is why you have children.

My son let me know he felt there was something not quite right about the neat bows I tied up all situations with. He, himself, couldn't quite figure out what the problem was. At first, I thought maybe he was just trying to irritate me. Happened before.

But, it got me thinking when an ugly development presented itself. It would be possible for a runner to be on base and also be due up as the batter. What to do? My bow came unraveled.

At first, and most simply, was the idea of a courtesy runner. This notion smelled so much like the designated hitter that it gave me a headache for which I had to take painkillers.

Later came the idea of the "T Ball solution" where everyone bats, even those on the bench. This idea required a three day retreat to overcome.

Sometimes, the simplest idea is the most elegant. Here it is: If a runner is on base and due up he or she is out BUT the batting team gets to decide if he or she is out at the bag they are on or at the plate. In other words, you could take the runner off the bag at the price of an out but, assuming it wasn't the third out, they would still get to bat.

This, of course, presents even more managerial opportunities both offensively and defensively.

For example, with five runners on and right base open to a right—handed runner (running counter-clockwise) and the runner on a corner base is "on-deck" you could walk a right-handed hitter to force the issue with less than two outs.

A keen manager might want to send up a left-handed hitter in this situation to preclude a walk and an automatic out.

Now that I am over the jitters of the unknown, I like envisioning some of the dynamics this situation might present. Bet Earl would also.

Double H

When I was a young man, still living on the farm with my folks, just about every Saturday during the summer, we would all go to Huron. At that time I had two interests.

One of them, of course, was music, and I finally managed to procure a second-hand phonograph. One of the first stops I would make was the Ben Franklin store to see what new records had come in. I remember the first one I purchased (that is to say, I remember purchasing a record but I don't remember which record.).

Anyway, I took my new treasure back to the car for safe keeping and, also, so I wouldn't have to drag it around with me all afternoon. I placed it on the rear deck behind the back seat and proceeded to my other area of interest. Those were the days when you could leave your keys in the car.

My other area of interest was blond and very pretty. She worked behind the counter at the Double H where I would go every Saturday, take a seat at the counter, order a butterscotch malt, hamburger, and French fries, and admire the view. I never screwed up the courage to speak to this beautiful young lady.

These two activities usually consumed my allowance so I would then head back to the car. This particular day, an especially warm one, I got back to the car before the rest of the family and found my new treasure melted.

Years later (and I have not confirmed this) I found out the blond person was named Cheryl Stoppelmoor who would eventually move to Hollywood and change her name, via marriage, to Cheryl Ladd.

At least I had good taste.

Farm Girl

When Tobey Russmann came home from the war he was ready to go back to the life he had known and just melt back into the community of Jessenland.

While in England, waiting for the big day, he spent his days off travelling the countryside and occasionally stopping at a sheep farm to talk with the farmer there. In this way he learned about other breeds and picked up animal husbandry tips to take back to his native North Dakota.

He came home to Ella, his bride, and a working interest in his father's sheep ranch. The first order of business was to build a small house on the farm for them to live in until his parents were ready to downsize and move out of the big farmhouse.

In time, this happened; hastened when Tobey and Ella had their first born child, a girl they named Signe. Later, after the three had moved into the big house, the family was completed when Darryl was born.

With Tobey's dad still helping on a reduced scale, the ranch thrived. They gradually moved into raising a registered breed and, thus, began a lot of paperwork, primarily handled by Ella. They made a good team, especially at lambing time in the spring.

As the children grew older and began to take on chores, the division of labor was traditionally gender specific. Darryl helped with the sheep chores and Signe showed a real knack for accounting and record keeping with her mom. Whenever she could, though, she ended up in the sheep barn and tried to be helpful. Like her mother, she was a real asset at lambing season.

The sheep ranch did well enough that the kids were able to earn allowances. With his, most of Darryl's money went into hunting gear and a second-hand reloader. Signe pursued her love of music by buying a good guitar and taking lessons in town. In time she became quite proficient.

As far as anyone knew, Darryl's dream was to grow up and live on the property and keep hunting. He was a quiet boy lost in his hobbies. Signe was just the opposite and quite outspoken in her hopes and dreams. As a teenager she became convinced her future was to go away to University, become a teacher and marry an engineer or doctor. They would live in Fargo and have a large house and a large family.

In 1965, Darryl got caught shining rabbits and was facing serious trouble. He had already had his favorite shotgun confiscated by the sheriff and a trial seemed imminent. Jessenland's only lawyer, Ronald Quist, arranged a plea bargain whereby Darryl would join the service by volunteering for the draft and the county would drop all charges. To Darryl, this sounded win—win.

He enlisted in the Army and was posted to Basic Training. It was there he became conscious of a piece of real estate called Viet Nam. Following completion of his training he was assigned this venue. He spent a few days at home before leaving. Signe was visibly upset that her loving brother was being sent off to an unheard of war. His dad, having survived D-Day, and his mother, having survived waiting and worrying about Tobey, were also quietly distressed. Darryl, however, seemed optimistic and gave all kinds of assurances.

With Darryl gone, Signe assumed most of his chores and became a worthy sidekick to her dad in all matters sheep. Her thinking was that this would last until Darryl came home by which time she would be ready to go off to college. It seemed like a good plan.

Sometimes, a different plan comes into play. About nine months into his tour of Viet Nam, Darryl was hit by sniper fire when he was out on a patrol. The slug was lodged near his spine and he was immobile. He was flown to Germany for surgery and months of therapy. Then, it became time to plan for him to return to North Dakota.

It took several weeks for everything to be ready for Darryl's homecoming. The house had to be retrofitted for a wheelchair. His room had to be moved to the main floor. Far removed from Washington, D. C., the local VA was of little help.

Signe cried when he came home. He was so helpless. Ella was in her element, however. She got to be a mother again to her favorite son. Attending to his needs became her new role while Signe, more and more, filled the role of assistant to her father. This went on for several months until, without warning, Ella died in her sleep one night.

Tobey declined an autopsy—what would it change?

Again, Signe's role changed. Putting off for the moment her wish to go to college, she now became chief housekeeper, attendant for Darryl, and helper for her dad. Lost in her work, the months, then years flew by.

Whenever she could find a few moments, she would play and sing for Darryl. One of his favorite songs was "Make Me Down a Pallet on Your Floor." He especially liked a version by Mississippi John Hurt.

Darryl, in the meantime, was starting to fail. He had less appetite and slept most of each day. Signe could see the change and seemed to sense what was coming.

Jessenland was located on a paved road a few miles from Highway 81 in the northeastern corner of the state. Except for church, there was no cultural outlet for its citizens. There wasn't even a movie house.

It was at a church function that she started to spend time with Marlin Quickstad, a farmer who had never married. Hard working, he ran his half section farm all by himself. He had a herd of twelve milk cows and sowed corn and small grains. He kept busy. He was seven years older than her but that didn't seem to matter. They talked, naturally enough, of farming.

Meantime, back at Tobey's place, Darryl acquired pneumonia and gave up the ghost at the age of thirty. Suddenly, it was just Tobey and Signe and Tobey was aging.

After Darryl's service, in the privacy of her own room, Signe took inventory. She was thirty-five and unmarried (and childless). It looked that, stretching before her was a life on the sheep ranch alone. This was not a prospect that appealed to her. She decided to talk to her dad about this.

Tobey proved to be a very understanding father; in fact, he seemed to have already begun the thought process for this event. They decided to scale down, and then sell the enterprise. The land was arable and virgin and there were any number of farmers that might want to own it for crops. They decided to visit an attorney to make the process and property clear of doubt.

With the successful sale of the farm and livestock, equipment, and other items, a joint trust fund was set up for the two of them which provided a nice income for each.

Now having a lot of time on her hands, Signe took a job with a local accountant in town. She enjoyed her job and the second income allowed for her to start planning her belated trip to college. She had not bothered to tell Marlin of this lifelong dream because it didn't seem to fit in with their budding plans. She was spending more and more time on his farm and could handle most of the chores including milking.

Eventually, her relationship with him began to gain traction and a spring wedding date was set. The upcoming event provided Jessenland with something to talk about and look forward over the end of winter.

As the big day drew near, things seemed to almost run on autopilot. This was fine for Marlin and planting season was now underway and he was spending very long days atop his tractor doing what farmers do. Signe, on the other hand, was a mess—she was, in fact, the autopilot, and doing her best to not bother Marlin with details.

The big day came and Tobey walked his radiant daughter down the aisle. Marlin looked handsome in a new but ill-fitting suit. After the ceremony and luncheon, the newlyweds retired back to Marlin's farm. Marlin immediately went to the bedroom and changed into overalls. Signe just stood there in shock. He came out of the bedroom, kissed her on her forehead and said "Can you handle the milking chores okay? I'll be home at six for supper."

As she stood there slack jawed, he breezed out of the house and out to his tractor. In her stunned state she went into the bedroom and changed into work clothes. She didn't know what to think. Almost in a trance, she took some steak out of the freezer for his supper. It would be two hours before milking time so she decided to rest for a bit. Unable to sleep, however, she got up and fussed around the house until time to go get the milk cows. After milking, she put the steak, some potatoes, and some vegetables into the oven to bake while she took a warm bath.

Sometimes a warm bath is life giving and that was how this felt. It recharged her and she felt renewed as she put on fresh clothes for supper. She set the table and, at five minutes after six, Marlin blew in for his repast. Not a big talker, he was almost silent, as if this was just another day in his bachelorhood. Meantime, Signe was doing a lot of processing. She tried to make conversation and he would answer her questions briefly but had no interest in leading the conversation.

After supper, he stood up, walked over to her and, again, kissed her on the forehead. "I don't know when I will be in—lots to do. I'll go as long as I can." With that, he was gone again.

The picture that was forming in Signe's mind was not the one she had envisioned when anticipating marriage. She could see he had been a bachelor so long he didn't even need a wife. And, truth to tell, she didn't need a husband so bad she would live like this. She took the suitcase she had planned on taking on their honeymoon and dumped it out. Putting some of her old things into the suitcase including her checkbook, she loaded the suitcase and her guitar into her car and headed for town. Geno's service station was still open so she filled the car with gas and headed westward. If her lifelong plan had been to be a teacher *and* a wife, she could at least get the teacher thing right and Ellendale had a teacher's college she had once been accepted to.

It was almost morning when she reached the outskirts of Ellendale. The motel flashing a Vacancy sign looked very inviting to her tired person. She took a room and slept for twelve hours. When she awoke, towards evening, she drove around the little college town until she found a "For Rent" sign on an apartment building near the college. She looked at the place, decided it was sufficient, and signed the paperwork. Tomorrow, Monday, she would find furnishings for it. Tuesday, she would go to the Admissions office and become a student.

Friday night she called Tobey with her new phone number and address. Afterwards, she poured herself a glass of milk and took out her guitar. Strumming and humming she began to softly sing

"Make me down a pallet on your floor."

"Make me down a pallet on your floor."

"Make me down a pallet soft and low."

"When I'm broke and I got no place to go."

She sang a few more verses, then, put the guitar away. After rinsing out the milk glass, she turned out the light and climbed into bed.

Gerrymeandering

This is definitely a "good old days" story but true, nonetheless.

A good friend and one of our senior card players had an experience that likely wouldn't happen today. As a young person, she was to start a new job with the Great Northern Railroad. At that time, this company had an office building in downtown Saint Paul.

On an adjacent block was the office building of the Northern Pacific Railroad Company.

On the appointed day, our friend showed up for work.

It wasn't until almost noon that it was discovered she went to the wrong building and had already put in half a day with the wrong company.

The wrong company then offered her employment and she put in over thirty years loyal service with Northern Pacific in all its incarnations.

Recently, she wasn't feeling well and ended up in the hospital where she subsequently passed away.

Makes me wonder: Did she go to the wrong hospital?

Muscle Memory

As the ball left my throwing hand, I was stunned to see it get only part-way towards first. And, the more I threw, the worse I got.

For a long time I had believed we die a little at a time. An organ here, a limb there. So it goes. But, I now see, for a lifetime athlete, one dies one skill at a time. First, the running slows for example.

As part of my recovery plan after my heart attack, I decided to play in an old man's church softball league. I hadn't played in years but, I guess I figured it must be like riding a bike. Come batting practice and I discovered I had no eye-hand coordination any more. I was swinging and missing. In slo-pitch! In all my life I only remember even one foul ball and no swings and misses in slo-pitch.

In thinking about this, I was reminded of Von McDaniel, a once shooting star in the St. Louis Cardinal pitching rotation. One day, for no explicable reason, his mechanics left him. He couldn't throw strikes any more—he couldn't get anyone out. He ended his baseball career as a third baseman in the minor leagues.

It comes to us all, some earlier than others but to us all nonetheless.

DumbWriter

In some sense, my books are about language, principally English. That is partially what gives me joy in writing.

In a past life I also did a lot of writing for my company. Much of what goes on in many workplaces is tied to oral history. When entities begin to structure and formalize procedures and other documents, this all changes. It is a serious cultural endeavor.

Often (*too* often) I would submit a written version of oral history to become a formalized corporate document and I would be told to "dumb it down." Usually this was an HR directive and, of course, usually I resisted. I would argue in vain that we had an opportunity to elevate the reading and language skills of the workforce.

This, it turns out, was only the tip of the iceberg.

Later, there would be arguments about having the documents in multiple languages. Pardon me for being a fossil here. This is the United States. We do not speak Swahili or Urdu as chief languages. This is supposed to be a melting pot. Let's get the people who don't speak English to hurry up and melt.

I bought a new printer today. I had to throw away half the documents because they were in other languages. We are not entering into a paperless society. In fact, we are killing trees at an even faster rate because of this misguided idea.

Anyway, the nice thing (very nice) about being a writer now is I can assume some intelligence on the part of the reader who, if he or she doesn't understand something, at least knows how to look it up. Finally, writing is fun.

Time's Up

Sophie was in the midst of beginning supper for herself and her husband, Marvin, when she felt a hand on her shoulder.

Right away, she knew what this was. She didn't even turn around. She had been expecting this for some time now. Her health was fading fast and it was becoming more and more difficult to shield it from Marvin.

"May I at least finish making supper for Marvin?" she asked.

"No, Sophie. It's time."

"May I go put on some more presentable clothes first?"

"Sophie—the garment the Lord has for you outshines anything you could possible have in your closet."

"Okay. So what do I do now?"

"I'll take care of it, Sophie."

As Sophie died and collapsed on the floor, she had a strange thought. She found herself wondering about the childhood game of jacks. She had been very good at jacks in her youth and wondered if there were jacks in heaven.

The Holy Escort lifted up Sophie and placed the body in the recliner. He then went into the kitchen and turned off the stove burners.

Then, they were off.

Eureka!

Part the First

Some things in life are just too big to disappear. Years ago I asked a brother-in-law, who was an elementary school principal at the time, if he had read "The Closing of the American Mind" by Allan Bloom. He responded with a loud guffaw and said "Are you kidding? I haven't read a book in twenty years."

It was truly an Archimedean moment.

It was all I could do to keep from shouting "I think I see the problem!"

Part the Second

Recently, I agreed to undergo the mother of all tests—a colonoscopy. I agreed because the doctor lied and said I would be unconscious.

On the day of the event, as I thought I would probably sleep through the thrill of a lifetime, the thrill came earlier than I expected. The doctor applied the coldest lube to be found on the entry point.

Instantly, I bi-located.

I had spent the previous three days totally emptying myself for this encounter. But when the doctor did this, I almost created a surprise just out of thin air.

"Not to worry" said the doctor. "It's room temperature."

The me that was clinging to the ceiling silently shouted:

"Yeah—right! If the freaking room is a refrigerator!"

Comes Around

Back in the early 1960s, my cousin's husband hired my brother, then about fifteen years old, to help with a procedure called blue-grass stripping. This is hard, hot, dirty work.

My brother got up early both days, packed a lunch, and went to work.

At the end of the second day, about ten o'clock in the evening, he came in the house, the job being done. He looked totally beat. He walked over to mother's dresser, pulled four wrinkled one dollar bills out of his jeans pocket, said "Here—I don't want it." And went to bed.

Over the years I have wondered about this. It calculates to maybe fourteen cents per hour for the total job. What I have wondered about is this: When the cousin's husband went home that night, was he chortling because he had basically stolen labor or was he feeling regret? No, not regret at his stinginess. Regret that he should have paid only three dollars or maybe two.

Maybe he should have tried to talk my brother into donating his time and labor as a good family gesture.

In later years, after my father stopped farming and rented out the arable portion of the farm, the cousin's husband would try to get my mom and dad to sell the farm to him at a sweetheart price to "keep it in the family."

As you can see, his idea of family is quite a bit different than most other people's. Fortunately, this didn't happen.

I would like to introduce you to my brothers. Both younger than me, the older of the two is one of my heroes. Unflappable, a soldier's calmness surrounds him—"This, too, shall pass" must be his driving thought.

The other is just a dry match away from incendiary outrage. Politics and religion will send him into incomprehensibility and the best you can do is wait out the storm and, then, change the subject. He is also a hero of mine.

Both gave up a large portion of their adult working lives to help our parents in their later years. Now, with both parents gone they find themselves stuck in that great example of right-to-work, South Dakota. No jobs to be had, shrinking towns, closing schools, aging demographics.

It was perhaps thirty years after the bluegrass episode that we decided, as a family, to sell the farm. We had all decided independently that the cousin's husband would not get it. If when the auction came (which took place by phone) the cousin's husband was the only bidder or high bidder, we would not sell it. Elephants are not the only ones with long memories.

What was really sad about this whole episode is the cousin is one of our favorite people and is not like her husband at all in those matters mentioned. When she talks family she is thinking people.

If I may be so bold as to channel Ben Franklin here: Save a buck today, lose hundreds of thousands tomorrow.

Brushes

Mostly, we go through life having direct contact only with other ordinary people like ourselves. Once in a while, though, we have a brush with celebrity, even if only tangential.

As a youth, our 4-H softball team was pretty good and one year we reached the state tournament. In our first game there (and, it turns out, our *only* game) we faced a pitcher named Feller. A great nephew, I think, of the hall of famer from Iowa.

My brother, our pitcher, pitched his heart out and so did our opponent. They won and my memory of that game that has been the most vivid was my brother taking the young Feller feller deep. I hope he (my brother) has a good memory of this day also.

Later, as an adult, I wound up in a mixed doubles kittenball tournament. Hitting a kittenball is like hitting a pillow. In these mixed team events, you play five females and five males. Usually these tournaments had very good players of both genders on the field.

One of the rules of this tournament was that you alternate male and female batters. A second, key rule was that, if you walked a male, the female coming up was walked automatically.

Batting third on a very windy day, I quickly had a 3 - 0 count with two runners on. I knew if I walked we would get a run because the woman following me in the batting order would gain the automatic walk.

Of course, the opposing pitcher, a woman who had to be less than five feet tall, managed to bring the count full.

As the next pitch left her hand it was obviously going to be way outside. I relaxed. Wind gust. Strike three.

We never recovered.

My lasting memory of that day was their manager, Steve Winfield, hitting the pillow over the fence.

Guess it runs in the family.

Dodger Blue(s)

As a very young boy, my goal in life was not to become a teacher or policeman or farmer, but to grow up and take over at shortstop for Peewee Reese on the Brooklyn Dodger baseball team. I reasoned this out very well. By the time I was ready, Peewee would be old and the timing would be perfect. (I look at this last paragraph now and realize that, while I knew Duke Snider's real first name was Edwin, I must have thought Peewee was Mr. Reese's given name.)

We had not one team in any pro sport to root for where we came from so we all had teams from faraway places. I became fixated on the Brooklyn Dodgers and, when they won their first World Series in 1955 and when some older kid stuck her head into our classroom and announced "The Dodgers won the World Series, I let out a whoop that got me sent to the hall.

Fortunately my mom was a baseball fan (a die hard Cardinal fan) and when I got home from school she gave me a vivid account of Sandy Amoros robbing Yogi Berra late in the game with a spectacular catch. I was hooked.

Then, in 1958, they moved to Hollywood. I know—it was really Los Angeles but in those days I equated them the same. I didn't know what to do. I was a Dodger fan but ambivalent about a change in venue. "Brooklyn Dodgers" sound so much better as a phrase than "Los Angeles Dodgers." For one thing, it is hard to reconcile a "dodger" with an angel. It's like a label that embodies both good and evil. I was perplexed.

So when they won another series in 1959 against the "Go-Go Sox, I was still not sure. Meantime, our neighbor, Minnesota, got the Twins. They have never had a chance with me even before the designated wussy. They were "American League."

This whole problem of relocation is relevant today. Here, in Minnesota we have an ultra-rich absentee owner of the pro football team trying to get the populace to build him a new glitzy playpen in the middle of an economic depression and using Los Angeles as a lever.

Los Angeles lost their team a few years ago to St. Louis. While still in Los Angeles, the Rams were oh-for-one in Superbowls. The Vikings are oh-for-four. Would the Vikings moving there be an improvement for Los Angeles who could now claim to be oh for five in the big one? I think not.

What is really instructive about this drama is this: Los Angeles has survived without a pro football team!

Still, I will always feel sorry for Brooklyn.

The Dodger thing gets worse by the minute. An ex-married couple is squabbling over who gets more of the Dodger pie while, meantime, the club heads toward bankruptcy.

But the real problem is this: The last two managers have been Yankees!

It is often said of Tommy Lasorda that he bleeds Dodger Blue. Do these two managers bleed Yankee Pin Stripe?

Simon Sings

"When I think back on all the crap I learned in high school..."
("Kodachrome"—Paul Simon)*

Paul Simon is right. I can think of three good examples.

Let's start with Christopher Columbus. I wonder if he discovered anything. He certainly didn't discover the United States. Yet, there is a whole cultural heresy built around this issue. It's even a holiday, for Heaven's sake! And, I hope the Pope will forgive me for pointing this out, but, the Knights of Columbus? Excuse me. When I think of the Knights of Columbus I think of a group of paunchy old men with swords and sashes wandering around wondering where they are (like Columbus must have done)!

And the whole idea that an entire continent already brimming with people is in need of discovering is absurd in the first place.

Then, there's George Armstrong Custer. West Point Wonder Boy. Who, early on, recognized the power and gullibility of the press. Remember being taught how he was massacred at Little Big Horn? Did any of you ever once hear the teacher tell you what his mission was? Or, at least what he *wanted* the mission to be? To kill or massacre first! He failed so we make him a hero. He wasn't a hero. Even his commander feared him to be a loose cannon.

Finally, there's the saga of the Lusitania. This was, ostensibly, a passenger ship plying the Atlantic. That's what I remember being told. What I wasn't told and, truth to tell, probably what the teachers weren't told, was the fact that we were also using it as a cover ship to transport armaments to Great Britain. Germany warned us to stop doing that or they would sink it. We didn't and they did. Another fine example of our government saying "To Hell with a few citizens." I'm sure someone in the war department did a benefit/cost analysis and gave the financial okay. Of course, our fine government denied this afterwards.

*"Kodachrome" lyrics. © Universal Music Publishing Group. Accessed 12 August, 2012.

I believe the subject ought to be called "mistory" rather than history. History it isn't. And, there are probably numerous other examples. Our sixteenth President comes to mind—someone called Lincoln. Ask the Sioux of Minnesota if he deserves the halo we give him. Same with JFK and the Bay of Pigs insurgents who had air cover withdrawn at the last moment leaving them sitting ducks.

The list goes on.

Dropout

Life in the gaggle was idyllic. The food was plentiful; water was abundant, nesting places all over, a wonderful lack of predators.

Donna and Duke and their fledgling daughter, Margaret, were thriving on the recently picked cornfield in southern Canada. In a week or so they would all lift off and head south for the winter. This would be a real test for Margaret and all the other young ones in the group but they were all strong and eager.

When the day came to leave, Leonard, a four-year old, was selected to lead off the formation for the first few hundred miles or so then to be relieved by Tony. It was a very noisy morning. All the parents would be in the opposite leg of the "V" from their child so they could keep an eye on them and the kid could look over and see them. It was a well-thought out strategy that had served for hundreds of years.

It was still dark as they all lifted off and headed south. Leonard would lead them to the Missouri flyway and then follow the river for the first leg. Toward sunup, Leonard led them toward the reservoir called Lake Sakakawea and found the outlet to the Missouri towards the eastern end of the lake. Things were going smoothly and everyone was keeping up.

Suddenly, explosions started popping all around. Leonard led them higher and the noise abated slightly but did not stop. Suddenly, Margaret drifted out of formation to the other leg and screamed in goose to her mother "Where's dad?"

Donna looked back and, sure enough, he wasn't there. Donna turned to her daughter and ordered, "Go back to your spot and stay with the flock no matter where it goes, understand?"

Margaret, who didn't really understand, shook her head and asked "What about you?"

Donna said "I have to go find him. I love you. Now go!"

Margaret said "I love you, too, mom." and half-heartedly drifted back to her spot in formation. She could see her mom dropping out of the vee and heading back. Then, she was gone.

A little while later Nola, one of the other mothers, flew alongside Margaret to try and console her and just generally check on Margaret's frame of mind. Nola told her that this sometimes happened but the flock must press on and everyone was important to the flock.

Meantime, Donna had dropped altitude and gained speed as she spiraled back over their itinerary with an eye out for Duke. Once again she heard the sound of gunfire and could even smell the smoke. She wasn't listening to the gunfire but was focusing on trying to hear Duke's distinctive honking below. She slowly glided along the edge of the waterway keeping a sharp lookout for him.

Ahead was a marshy area that looked safe so she aimed for it honking as she flew. To her total surprise, she heard an answer from Duke and she beamed in on the location coming to a soft splash landing near where his honking came from.

Safely in the water and hidden in the reeds, she honked for him. Eventually they found each other and she gave him the once over. Fortunately, he had been high enough that the pellets had almost spent their energy by the time they found him. He had some imbedded in his chest and two had pierced his right wing leaving small holes.

She patiently pecked at the shot in his chest area until they had worked loose and fell out. All the while, soft goose-chatter was going on. She decided for both of them that they would spend a couple of days hidden in the reeds and then leave by night after he had a chance to do some healing. In a way, she was in her glory and it was as if she was tending another gosling.

Margaret, ever the obedient child, stayed with the flock as it bore southward. Even though her heart was heavy with feelings of unknown description, she wanted to please her mother.

And, she had met Corey.

Day by day, the flock extended their journey away from the North. Food and water were plentiful. The shooting had almost stopped. As the river shifted eastward, they migrated likewise heading for delta country. By now, not a single goose was carrying fat.

Margaret and Corey managed to fly together most days and spent most of their earth-bound time in each other's company. Gradually, the unnamed pain in Margaret's heart dissolved.

Up north, Duke and Donna knew it was time to go. They had made a few short trial run flights to test out the healing and Duke was pretty tolerant of any pain. This flying at night was going to be testy, they knew. Duke felt that they would only be doing this for a couple of days though.

On a chilly, starlit night, they silently took off. The higher they climbed, the chillier it was so they kept at a low altitude. It took about a half hour for them to find a rhythm and pace both were comfortable with. With the starlight they could follow the river pretty closely. Toward four a.m., they alighted in the river and sought some cover.

They followed this routine for two more nights and days when the weather seemed to be a little balmier. As they flew under starlight, they hummed a tune:

Into the night

The tardy pair

Working hard

In crisper air

To South! To South!

Before the big snow

Keep flapping, Keep flying

To the delta we go!

It was an old goose tune composed many migrations ago, its author long forgotten.

Somewhere over Nebraska or maybe Kansas, Duke took another header. By now they were flying in daylight and Donna saw the whole episode as he fell. She followed him on down but his landing was ugly. In fact, if he were not already dead it would have been fatal. Some of the shell shot had hit a vital organ and now he was gone.

Donna, of course, couldn't know what had really happened but she did understand he was gone- that she was now alone. She spent the rest of the day and night next to Duke but, by morning, knew it was time to go it alone.

Flying solo, she could go a little faster even though she would be her own windbreak. She easily put miles behind her as she honed in on the Delta. By the time she was cruising past Kansas City and drifting southeastward, the main body of the flock was already in their homepatch enjoying the warm weather and resting up.

Margaret and Corey were inseparable and starting to make plans. He was a year older than Margaret and relished being her beau. In fact, all over the homepatch, couples were pairing up for spring.

Donna's homecoming was the cause for the social event of winter with the geese. Margaret's sadness at not seeing her father was balanced with having her mother nearby to talk with and share her new happiness. Donna readily approved. But, because she herself was alone now, she deliberately chose a place on the periphery of the group. Unformed plans were settling in her fine head and she needed solitude to work them out.

The winter thus passed and it was time for the flock to go back to Canada. Donna had come to a decision. She would stay behind this year. Leonard and the others tried to dissuade her but to no avail.

When departure day came, she bid farewell to Margaret and Corey admonishing them to be careful. Corey gave her a peck and off they went.

Late, in Spring in lower Canada, a gander was hatched whom the parents named Duke. He had the brash swagger of someone named Duke. He grew quickly into a handsome young goose.

His parents, his mother especially, were very proud and looked forward to presenting him to his grandma.

Joe M.

I recently attended the funeral of a man I worked with over twenty years ago. Why do we attend funerals of people we haven't seen or heard from in this long? Because, they have made an indelible impression on us.

As I was sitting alone in a wing chair in the corner of the room at the funeral home where Joe was laid out, I began to reflect more on this question. What was it about him that made him so memorable?

He was a quiet, polite man. In the ten years or so I worked with him, I never heard him raise his voice or utter any profanity. There was never an unkind word from him. Yet, he was a very intelligent person who must have had opinions.

I realized, sitting there, that it was his unobtrusive manner that made him memorable. He was not loud or garish. Modest, almost to a fault, he was so self-effacing as to almost deny even his own existence.

So many of the so-called role models we encounter in life are, of course, just the opposite. Loud, "Look at me!" Famous. Perhaps skilled in some physical endeavor. Perhaps a movie or television "personality" although, there is little personality there these days. Maybe, God forbid, a politician.

Joe was none of these. But, in the end, maybe that was what made him the archetypical role model. Humble, of service to others.

On the day he died, Joe—retired all of four months—had a doctors appointment for his eyes. He always walked or took the bus. On this day the bus didn't come so he returned home to phone the doctor's office. As he was talking with the receptionist he said "Excuse me for a moment." The young person on the other end of the line could hear coughing for about thirty seconds, then silence.

She then called 911 and the paramedics were on the scene quickly but Joe was gone.

Thinking back, how like Joe to say, "Excuse me." And then go die.

NCFF

> "Kake noticed a small, thick rope sticking out of the corner of the big paper bag. It was kind of orange with some black also. He tugged the rope and more came sliding out. It was now evidently striped orange and black. Still curious, he gave a big yank and a tiger —a very hungry tiger—came tumbling out. The first thing she saw was Kake."
>
> From "The Death of Kake" by Agatha Grisham (unpub.)

There is an entity that supposedly oversees collegiate activities. Unfortunately, it now thinks its role is as a social behavior monitor and, in even that role it fails miserably.

There is a sports team in North Dakota called the Fighting Sioux. Even if you erased from our history all Indian movies starring Ronald Reagan—not a bad piece of history rewrite—we would still be left with a library of conflict movies involving the U. S. Calvary and the Sioux people. I live in Minnesota where Lincoln had almost three dozen Sioux hanged simultaneously. The conflict was real.

Yet, this august (some might say April) body has decided the name "Fighting Sioux" has to go. Not the "Fighting Irish" or the "Fighting Illini" even though, to the best of my knowledge, we have never been at war with either Ireland or Illinois. It's selective historical rewrite.

Now comes an event so disgusting and so hard to stomach yet, the NCFF is no where to be found. At Penn State, child abuse and coverups go hand in hand. But, because this involves a vaunted football program with an iconic coach, it is ignored. If there was *ever* an opportunity to take a stance involving social behavior, this is it.

The NCFF needs to grab this tiger by the tail and show some huevos. Can money be so important you taint your organization through inaction? I have heard some suggestions to shut this program down for a while—say five years or more. I don't care if they shut it down until Sandusky is released. Dead or alive.

Ends and Odds

Is it just me or has the whole world become an economic raisin?

***

I may be no Hemingway but I am earnest.

***

It is a valid economic indicator, trust me. My wife and I would occasionally find a coin on the sidewalk or in the parking lot but we haven't seen even a penny for months now.

***

Struggles make you strong. Snuggles make you human.

***

Another valid economic indicator: When you reach my age you tend to read obituaries. Lately, more and more of them contain the phrase "There will be no service."

***

In life we make choices. I have tasted prune juice. I choose constipation.

***

One of the things I love about God is that he ignores the weathercasters.

***

In Heaven there is no bier.

***

The bigger the haystack, the harder it is to find the needle.

***

Of local interest only: Recently declassified Federal documents show that, originally, the Twin Cities International Airport was going to be built in Maplewood. The plan was scrapped, however, when local leaders insisted there be a roundabout halfway down the runway.

***

Old Wives Tale. Whenever I hear this expression I am confused. Is it the tale or the wife that is old?

***

Friends and family that know I write think it is the road to riches. I just received my first royalty check from my first book. My bride and I are now considering buying a house.

A bird house.

***

I recently had some surgery. Many friends and family who knew it was coming wished me luck.

Gee—I was really hoping it wouldn't come down to that.

***

Perhaps another valid economic indicator—or a sign of the apocalypse: My wife recently had her wallet stolen—in a second hand store!

Nuances

Last Stop

I didn't expect to be here
Among the walking dead.
My children tell me it's okay;
I'm jumbled in my head.

I sometimes leave the burner on.
I sometimes fail to zip..
I'm walking slower than I did
I may need a new hip.

My lovely bride left earlier
To Heaven she did go.
It's been hard to be alone.
I guess that it must show

I'll make the best of this
And try not to complain.
It's where everybody wants me.
Guess I won't go home again.

Demarcation

Of the line that separates good from bad
I have fought on both sides.
A worthy soldier for my pay.

It is true the Devil can blur the line
So one is not sure.
But, in my heart, I am to blame.

Mostly I knew what I was doing
And wrong it was.
Yet, I carried forth in sin

Will my time on the good side help?
Are the accounts even?
Do I get a credit score that matters?

I know the outcome, the reward for me
As for anyone
Is dependent on mercy.

Can I be forgiven my mistakes?
He knows my heart
And that alone suffices.

Pride and Joy

Is this our son
Running up and down the floor?
My gosh, he's fast. Look at him run!
My gosh, he's good. Look at him score!

Is this our daughter
Who brought home all these "As"?
She'll be a doctor
One of these days.

The Lord really blessed us
When He lent us these two.
It will be tough to let them go.
But it's something we must do.

So let us enjoy them now
And help them while we can.
She'll too soon be a woman
As he will be a man.

Goose P**p

Sheesh! This golf course is a mess!
Why can't geese fly south for the summer?

I used to think I would love to be a goose
Flying so high.
Above my shotgun's range.
Rubbing it in, I suppose, to the ducks.

I loved their sense of timing
And I tried to understand their honks.
They sounded so happy
When they landed in the corn field.

Searching for leftovers.
Ever on alert.
Their goal, I'm sure,
Was to get everyone there safely.

There were lessons in group behavior,
Lessons in fidelity,
Lessons in followership,
But, we had other agenda.

RED VELVET LOVE

Your perfume leaves just a trace
But enough to entice me.
I follow the trail up the stair
And find you letting down your hair.
You smile at my desperation
As we start with an embrace.

For years this has been our way
Of saying the magic words.
Of starting the fire.
Lovingly, we conspire
To please each other
And bring sweet closure to our day.

I still can't believe how I can
Get lost in your red velvet love.
A gift of incalculable worth
Abiding at Heaven on Earth.
How did you choose me
To be your ever grateful man?

ACOLYTE

She carried many things
Inside her heart.
Where would we be
If she had not said "Yes?"

She watched Him grow,
Internalizing fate,
Painfully accepting
What must be.

When His time came
She understood.
Now Cana was the place
And water played a role.

Water often played a role
(See John the Baptist).
She became a disciple
And, still, His mother.

At the end, she was there.
Perfect closure;
Perfect understanding
Of a child's life.

TARNISHED MAN

Blessings on thee, Golden Girl
Laughing eyes and endless curl.
Center of my Earthly life.
Now my sweetheart; soon, my wife.

How I love thee! How I care!
You're the answer to my prayer.
When our life on Earth is done
A better life will start its run.

One to last eternity.
Me with you and you with me.
Then, God's great mysteries will unfurl
For Tarnished Man and Golden Girl.

Bubble Bath

The bubbles make a hissing sound
As they conspire to hide you in the foam.
A perfect defense made of air
Whose sweet aroma permeates our home.

Sometimes the things that we hold dear
May hold a smallish pricelessness to pay
Yet, pay a mighty dividend and
Help to wash away the troubled day.

So, sit and soak and sooth the tired and sore.
Relax and listen to the cleansing slosh.
Tomorrow is another battling day
Enjoy your well-earned respite as you wash.

Adrift

Sometimes I feel so unwanted.
Is it because I am?
Often I feel unheard.
Do I now bore you?
You frequently go to confession
Then, come home and start over.
Do you see a pattern here?

This endless conflict
Is wearing me down.
I find it less easy to care.
But I remember the words:
"For better or worse."
And I hang in there
Hoping things will change.

You say we've nothing in common.
How can this be after eighteen years?
I am a millstone
That's chained to your heart.
The rock of Sisyphus.
I 'm sorry I am such a burden.
I am dying as fast as I can.

Hard Times

The poverty gnaws
Like a dog at a bone.
Paycheck to paycheck
Is all hope now gone?

Sometimes, when I'm low
And I want to concede
You give me the heart
To do what I need.

Still the spirit will sag
As the trial drags on.
The American Dream
Now a nightmare too long.

People can't find jobs.
Homes go on sale.
Bankers get bonuses.
Too big to fail.

Forget about college;
Don't plan on success.
You're right to the brass ring
Is caught up in the mess.

Plan on apartments
And temp jobs for now.
Who knows what the answer?
Nobody knows how.

But bluff and bluster
Still carry the day.
We have the debates
Where there's nothing to say.

The politicos posture
And promise great things.
But truth in politics
Is a pig with wings.

Fight or Flight

Lately, I have been thinking
About letting go.
Not of possessions,
Or people,
But of life.

I try to imagine
What it is like
To not breathe
Or think
Or care.

I wonder if I would resist
The challenge.
Or is it a reward?
Would the real me
Emerge in all its rage?

My parents were wonderful
Examples of passivity
At death.
A calm acceptance
A lesson.

Squall

Hurricane is coming
Category four.
Cover all the windows;
Batten down the door.

Gas up all the vehicles.
Stock up on supplies
In case the siege is lengthy.
I'm told that this is wise.

Gather in the family.
Listen to it roar.
Give thanks for your safe haven
While the storm is at the door.

Think about the homeless
With no place to hide away.
They will huddle under bridges.
With no choice—they have to stay.

Hot Cold Hot

Unnamed woman you are
The essence of erotic fire
Your beauty brings me blindly to
The apex of desire

When I approach you softly
Seeking what is nice
I find a creature smiling
But who acts as if she's ice

Is it in your nature then
To confuse and hurt me so
Are you aware your power
To get me high or low?

I think about you always
Whether night or whether day
Do you ever have such thoughts of me
Do you wonder what I'd say?

Unnamed woman you are
The essence of erotic fire
Your beauty brings me blindly to
The apex of desire

Exiting

Drop the curtain to the stage
And lead me to the wings.
My act is over. I now go
To more important things.

I've told my jokes and sung my songs
And danced as best I could.
I've made some friends and lost some friends
And, mostly, I've been good.

The judgment that awaits me
I can only win through grace.
God's mercy my defender
His forgiveness wins my race.

Bridle Sweet

The horse's name is Thunder
He can run at quite a pace.
I got him at a claiming race
For horses three and under.

He likes his oats, he loves his hay.
He doesn't mind the reins.
It doesn't please him that he trains.
He'd rather romp and play.

The day will come his race is run.
Til then I just enjoy.
My fire-breathing equine toy
Who ran 'cause it was fun.

Torque

It has come to this:

We bend and twist each other's words
To suit our righteous songs.
To make us out as victims.
To justify our wrongs.

Agreement seldom happens.
Disputation takes the day.
We carry hurts inside us
That just won't go away.

What happened to togetherness
When love was truly there?
When we listened to each other
And we eagerly did share?

Now it's all been ripped asunder
Tis where doubt and anger live.
We're both so trapped inside the lie
And neither wants to give.

This is a case where we both lose.
Consider what we had.
The Devil must be laughing
To see us act so bad.

Needs Music

WHISPERING

Over and Over again, My Love, I've told you how I feel.
Hoping to "earn" your love, even if I have to steal.
It isn't working, I can see; been whispering into the wind.
Like a voice in the bewilderness I find I'm alone again

I've poured all that I am to you—have nothing left to give
I can't recharge all by myself, that's not the way to live.
A person needs loving in return, or their own love runs dry.
It's a painful process, take my word, I've no more tears to cry.

And so I walk away from this—this love I thought was true.
And, in the end, it means I fear, I walk away from you.
I must survive. I do believe God will bring me love again
Until that time I'm silent—no more whispering into the wind.

Panhandler Blues

"Mister, may I have a dime? I need to call my dad."
"When calls were just a dime, young man, your dad was just a lad."
"Would you have a dollar, sir? My car ran out of gas,"
"A dollar buys a quart these days; enough to mow some grass."

The math is so confusing, the decisions are a hoot.
There's no one left accountable—authority is moot.
Our printing press is so well oiled,
Our reputation so darn soiled,
You can't hatch chicks when the eggs are boiled.
The emperor's in his birthday suit!

"I'd like a grant—I feel a solar business onus"
"Here—take it all but first of all be sure you get a bonus."
"May I have a million, Prez? I want to build some cars."
"Here's a billion. Make sure your factory's in India or Mars."

The math is so confusing, the decisions are a hoot.
There's no one left accountable—authority is moot.
Our printing press is so well oiled,
Our reputation so darn soiled,
You can't hatch chicks when the eggs are boiled.
The emperor's in his birthday suit!

KETTLE. BELL RUNG.

She threw the kettle at me
When I walked through the door.
It hit me on my cranium
I fell upon the floor.

"Why'd you go and do that?'
I asked in headache haze.
"Perhaps you didn't realize
That you've been gone for days."

"I was with a friend who's ailing."
I explained as there I laid.
"Your friend had best be dead by now."
"The piper must be paid."

"Empty out your pockets Chump"
"And don't give me no stall."
I did as she demanded
Didn't think ahead at all.

A casino chip was in the mix
Of treasures on the floor
"Your friend's a loser also"
As she laid on me the score.

"From now on I get the money"
"And you get what I decide."
"You'll come home from work each evening"
"And you'll stay home with your bride."

"We will go to church on Sundays."
"We will go and see my folks."
"You will give up golf and fishing."
"You will give up dirty jokes."

Now, I am a good boy
And I do as wifey wants
But, I'm making plans to claim again
My favorite secret haunts.

I've hid the kettle in the barn
And readied all my toys
I'm using my vacation
To enjoy the good *old* boys.

She'll think I'm going to work today
But, fishing I will go.
Then call to say I'm working late
And so the week will go.

Rockets

I don't play pocket aces any more.
This world gives me no certainty like it did in days before.
The woman that I love has left and slammed my happy door.
I don't play pocket aces any more.

I believed her when she said "I do" and, maybe then, she did
I believed her when she told me she was mine.
I lived my life with her beside like it would never end.
I closed my eyes as if I was a man whose eyes were blind.

I never saw it coming, I played the utter fool.
In love with her; believing she was likewise loving me.
And now, my ex-best friend and her are gone forever more
It's solitaire for losers where the ante's always free.

I don't play pocket aces any more.
This world gives me no certainty like it did in days before.
The woman that I love has left and slammed my happy door.
I don't play pocket aces any more.

Dry Hole
(For the folks at Mammoth Resource Partners)

There is no oil or gas in ol' Kentucky.
Don't listen to the salesmen when they call
With voice adrip of honest down homism
Assuring you that they're the best of all.

They tell you they're the ones with integrity.
A new approach for investors at this time.
"We even invest in our own wells." they say
"Those other guys don't" they add "and that's a crime."

You get your daily updates on the web.
"Strong smell of oil" or "Maintenance" an entry said
"We've hit chert"—a great sign we are told
WTF—Are we drilling for oil or arrowheads?

The president of the company, (who's oh for fourteen)
Goes on tube because he's PhD.
"Invest in energy" he rails and rails
"You can someday be as rich as me."

The urge to sell this must be congenital.
Lie roll off the tongue like no one really cares.
"I think we're going to hit a cavern."
Kentucky come-ons so you buy more shares.

There is no oil or gas in ol' Kentucky.
Don't listen to the salesmen when they call
With voice adrip of honest down homism
Assuring you that they're the best of all.

Wait For You

On the first day of school
I fell in love with thee
Big school
You never noticed me

On the last day of school
Many years have passed
I'm still in love with you
In love irons I've been cast

I wait for you
I wait for you
Please hear my screaming heart
I wait for you

You go off to college
Far, far away
I get a job here at home
Come back soon, I pray

When you come back
I still see you
Even though you've changed
All I can do

Is wait for you
I wait for you
Please hear my screaming heart
I wait for you

You're getting married
And, sadly, not to me
Someone else is living
Where I want to be

How do I go on
This empty life of mine
All these years I've waited
Were just a waste of time

I wait for you
I wait for you
Please hear my screaming heart
I wait for you

About the Author

As stated in the previous work (*Rack and Wruin*), Rudyard Thurber is a pen name. This is his last work. The first book was a lark and kind of fun to write. This one has become more like work and, since the real author is retired, I wish to stay retired.

But, you never know. It never occurred to me when I was writing the first one that there would be a second.

So, if there is a next book, it will have a different partner. I have enjoyed the company of Mr. Thurber immensely. I am currently taking applications for the next one just in case. In fact, I have already interviewed one such applicant, that unique senior rapper, Bobbin Raye Ballou. I have included the interview for your own evaluation and recommendation.

Enjoy and thanks.

Interview of Bobbin Raye Ballou
(Transcribed from the oral original)

RUDYARD THURBER: "Hello, Mr. Ballou, it is a pleasure to meet you. I am Rudyard Thurber at your service."

BOBBIN RAYE BALLOU: "Nice to meet you Mr. Service."

RUDYARD THURBER: "No, I am Mr. Thurber."

BOBBIN RAYE BALLOU: "Oh, sorry, Mr. Herbert."

RUDYARD THURBER: "Mr. Ballou, I understand you describe yourself as a senior rapper, is that correct?"

BOBBIN RAYE BALLOU: "Yes, that is my official title down at Wal-Mart."

RUDYARD THURBER: "Your official title at Wal-Mart?"

BOBBIN RAYE BALLOU: "Yes. I started out as a general rapper but then got promoted to senior rapper."

RUDYARD THURBER: "How many rappers do they have at Wal-Mart anyway?"

BOBBIN RAYE BALLOU: "Well, there's Agnes and Larry and me."

RUDYARD THURBER: "My goodness, it must get fairly musical there."

BOBBIN RAYE BALLOU: "Poor Agnes, she thought she should have been the one promoted to senior rapper."

RUDYARD THURBER: "So, do you each cover a section of the store rapping away?"

BOBBIN RAYE BALLOU: "And, Larry, of course never had a chance."

RUDYARD THURBER: "So, all three of you sing rap?"

BOBBIN RAYE BALLOU: "Sing? Don't be silly. I couldn't carry a tune in a bucket."

RUDYARD THURBER: "What is your best selling record?"

BOBBIN RAYE BALLOU: "I think the one about a dark moon did real well."

RUDYARD THURBER: "I meant, 'What was your best selling rap record?'"

BOBBIN RAYE BALLOU: "I probably wrapped Michael Jackson records the most."

RUDYARD THURBER: "Michael Jackson wasn't a rapper."

BOBBIN RAYE BALLOU: "Well, I wouldn't know about that. He probably hired someone to do it for him."

RUDYARD THURBER: "Let me try again. Have you ever cut a record?"

BOBBIN RAYE BALLOU: "No. Why would I cut one up?"

RUDYARD THURBER: "But, you claim to be a rapper."

BOBBIN RAYE BALLOU: "Well, that is my job title. I also can sell paint and hardware."

RUDYARD THURBER: "Please name me one rap song you are famous for."

BOBBIN RAYE BALLOU: "Rap song? We don't have songs for wrapping presents."

RUDYARD THURBER: "Wrapping presents? You mean you wrap presents for Wal-Mart?"

BOBBIN RAYE BALLOU: "Why, yes. What did you think I did?"

RUDYARD THURBER: "You mean you have never heard of Eminem?"

BOBBIN RAYE BALLOU: "Of course I have heard of M and Ms. Although, to be honest, my wife is the one who really likes them."

RUDYARD THURBER: "Eminem is a rapper."

BOBBIN RAYE BALLOU: "What she really likes are M and M Blizzards at Dairy Queen."

RUDYARD THURBER: "Rap is a form of music."

BOBBIN RAYE BALLOU: "Personally, I like the Snickers Blizzards."

RUDYARD THURBER: "So, you've never heard of or wrote or recorded rap music?"

BOBBIN RAYE BALLOU: "Sometimes the Snickers nougat gets stuck to my partial. Does that ever happen to you?"

RUDYARD THURBER: "I can see we should change the subject."

BOBBIN RAYE BALLOU: "Okay. What church do you go to?"

RUDYARD THURBER: "No—I'm the interviewer—I will change the subject."

BOBBIN RAYE BALLOU: "We go to the Church of the Everlasting Fundraiser."

RUDYARD THURBER: "No, we will change the subject to relevant experience."

BOBBIN RAYE BALLOU: "Every week, there is a second collection."

RUDYARD THURBER: "Excuse me. . ."

BOBBIN RAYE BALLOU: "Or a special speaker to motivate us."

RUDYARD THURBER: "What are some examples of your writing?

BOBBIN RAYE BALLOU: "Sometimes I get the feeling we go to church at a public television station."

RUDYARD THURBER: "Have you written any books or articles?"

BOBBIN RAYE BALLOU: "One of these Sundays, I half expect them to trot out an old folk trio to strum every last dollar out of us."

RUDYARD THURBER: "Well, Mr. Ballou, this interview is about over."

BOBBIN RAYE BALLOU: "Say, do you like this suit?"

RUDYARD THURBER: "I will let you know about the opportunity."

BOBBIN RAYE BALLOU: "It was 'Buy one—get one free.'"

RUDYARD THURBER: "Yes, it's a nice suit."

BOBBIN RAYE BALLOU: "I can wear the other one for a second interview."

RUDYARD THURBER: "I'm sure that won't be necessary."

BOBBIN RAYE BALLOU: "It's brown. My wife likes brown."

RUDYARD THURBER: "Thank you for your time, Mr. Ballou. I'll be in touch."

BOBBIN RAYE BALLOU: "Okay. Thank you Mr. Sherbert."

www.ingramcontent.com/pod-product-compliance
Lightning Source LLC
LaVergne TN
LVHW020937090426
835512LV00020B/3395